DINOSAURS
COLORING BOOK

Cheryl Wallace

This book belongs to:

____

____

____

Dinosaurs
Spinosaurus

Dinosaurs
Baryonyx

Dinosaurs
brachiosaurus

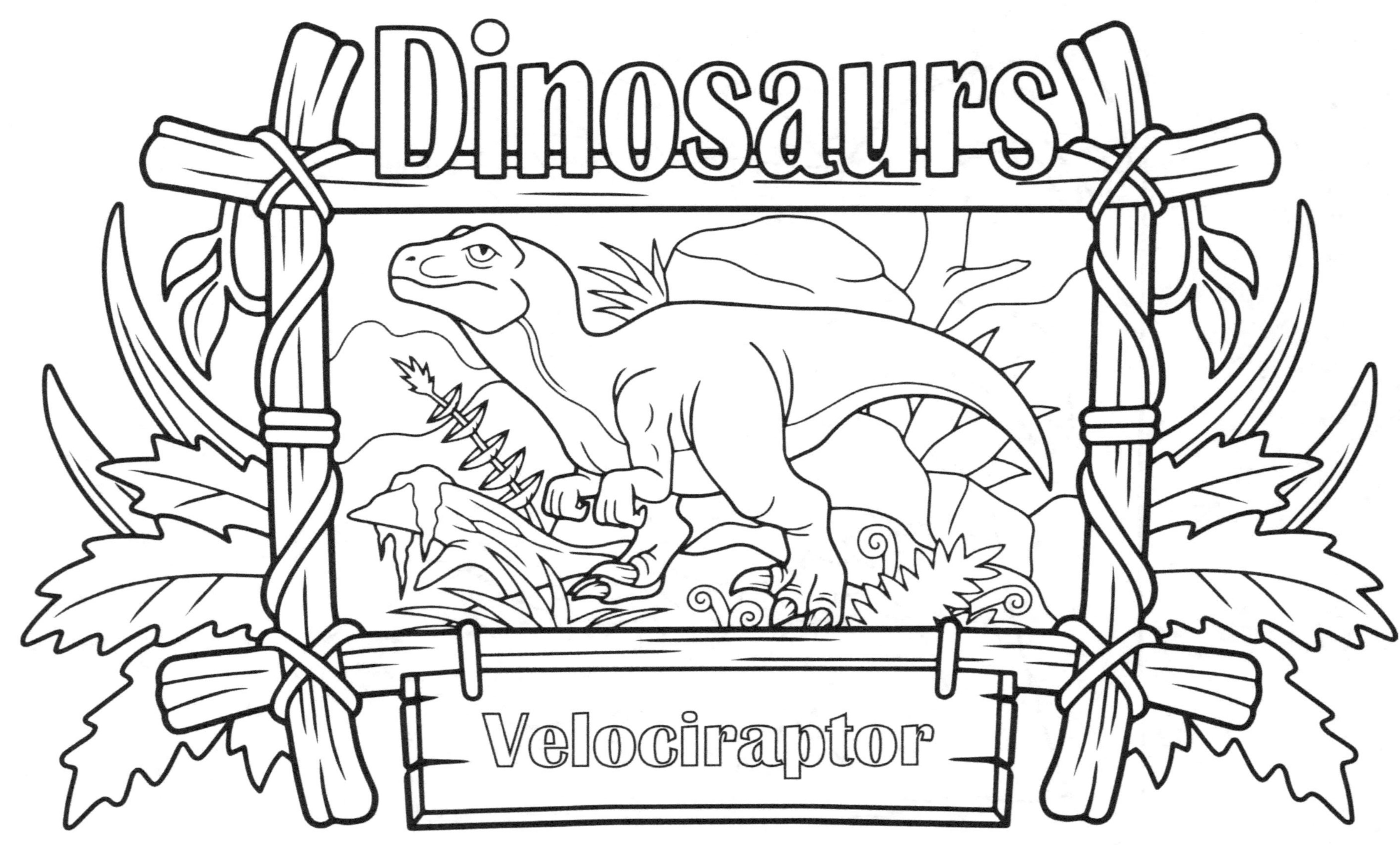

Dinosaurs
Velociraptor

Dinosaurs
Triceratops

Dinosaurs
Stegosaurus

Dinosaurs
Triceratps

9 798553 554750